Acknowledgements

It is fitting that Coralie Castle and Carrie Domogalla are listed on the title page; without their contributions this would be a quite different book. Coralie Castle, a cookbook author of long standing, did her best to emend, correct, and clarify the recipes. Carrie Domogalla of Illuminations Press secured contributions, tested recipes, checked sources and did many of the things necessary to make the work ready for publishing.

I need to give extra thanks to Ralph Tucker for his ideas and recipes and his untiring devotion to snails and the Snail Club.

I am most grateful to the contributors. Their enthusiasm for the project has been heartening and their recipes have added much to the book.

Some of the recipes are original, others came from sources unknown. Wherever possible, credits have been given. Any similarity to a recipe already published is purely accidental and unintentional.

Finally, thanks to Gene Dekovic for giving form to the work with his design and photography and for shepherding it through the many steps the work must take before reaching your hands.

Frances Herb

St.Helena, California
July 15, 1990

Contributors

Edward Borg—*Escargots Carmel-by-the-Sea*—and his wife, Sue, live in Carmel, California. Both retired, they spend much of their time in social work and in entertaining in their home.

George Francisco—*Coho Salmon Stuffed with California Snails*—is the chef at the *Mount View Hotel* in Calistoga, California. When food and the Mount View are the subjects, George's enthusiasm and energy level are impressive. And his cuisine is equally so: imaginative compositions of fresh ingredients, prepared with a light touch. His prior work includes San Francisco restaurants: Stars, Fog City Diner and Cafe Claude.

Piper Johnson—*Escargot Quiche Piper Johnson*—are husband/wife team, chef Nicholas Johnson and Terri Piper, operating *Piper-Johnson Catering* in Calistoga, California. Committed to quality California French cuisine, using fresh Northern California products, they emphasize pairing fine wines and fine foods in tasteful presentations.

Jeff & Sandee Lawson—*Snail Ranch Snails*—operate the *Snail Ranch* in Visalia, California, and ship their fresh snails over a large area. Jeff and Sandee's recipe was used at the Great Snail Festival in Southern California and people lined up for more. They can be reached at (209) 734 4532 or visited at their ranch in Visalia.

Mary Stewart—*Fresh Snails in Jumbo Pasta*—owner of *E'lite California Fresh Escargot & Caviar* prepares and markets a variety of flavors of escargot caviar as well as fresh snails. The caviars are packed in small jars and can be used as garnish from appetizers to dessert. E'lite's offerings were another big hit at the Great Snail Festival. Mary can be reached at (209) 568 1508 in Strathmore, California.

Ralph Tucker—*Poppers, Snail Fritters with Tomato Sauce, and many other recipes*—is the founder and President of The Snail Club of America. The club periodically publishes a newsletter for the members to exchange information, recipes, etc. He, and the club, can be reached at 187 North Duke Avenue, Fresno, CA 93727.

Contents

Snail-stuffed Mushroom Caps, p. 29

1. Catching the Snails

An old recipe for rabbit stew began with the admonition, "First you catch the rabbit." How does one catch snails?

In temperate areas of California and other parts of the United States the common snail, the *Helix aspersa,* can be found in abundance in gardens and orchards during favorable weather conditions. To turn these snails into tasty dishes is not difficult. These are the same snails, the *Petit Gris,* that the French have long esteemed as the culinary delight, *escargot.*

During times of relatively high humidity, such as warm, misty mornings or evenings, the snails will be found crawling on lawns, sidewalks, or vegetation. They can be easily scooped into a basket or box with a perforated top. One should select the largest, most active ones in areas that are free of any pesticides or poisonous sprays.

Not everyone lives in such bountiful areas. Fortunately, now there are growing numbers of enthusiastic individuals who are marketing snails raised under controlled conditions to provide the highest quality of product. Eventually, this product will become more widely available. In the meantime, neophyte snail cooks can enjoy these recipes using canned snails.

The best way to ensure a future supply of fresh, tender, tasty snails is for the consumer to continue to ask for and insist on getting the best quality possible. A good comparison that can be made between fresh and canned snails is the difference between fresh and canned vegetables. Canned vegetables have their use, but the fresh are much, much better.

2. Purging

The collected snails can be confined in a clean environment, such as a plastic bucket with a wire-mesh cover, and given a diet of dampened corn meal and clean water. The snails should be kept thus for five to seven days, the food and water being changed as necessary to ensure good sanitation. The light, cornmeal color of the feces will indicate when the snails are completely purged of any undesirable material.

3. Parboiling

The purged live snails are dropped into rapidly boiling water to which a bay leaf and the juice of a lemon have been added. After the water has returned to a full boil, the snails are cooked for 8 to 10 minutes. Shaking the pot occasionally will reduce the development of any foam. The snails should be drained and then covered with cold water so they can be handled.

To remove the snail from the shell, grasp it in the left hand with the fleshy foot exposed. Slip a skewer, such as a round tooth pick, through this muscle, and, with a twist of the wrist in a counter-clockwise motion, unscrew the snail intact from its shell. Since it is a very flavorable part of the meat, the tortillon, which is in fact the liver-pancreas, should be left on it. The snails are then ready for use in any of a great many different, all delicious, recipes.

If one wishes to parboil more snails than are needed, the extras can be successfully frozen for future use. After the snails are removed from the shell, arrange them separately on a cookie sheet, and freeze quickly. Then selected amounts can be sealed in separate plastic bags. The frozen snail meat can be thawed as needed in room-temperature water for a few minutes while other preparations are being made. Of course, as with other ingredients, fresh is better.

4. Cleaning the Shells

Bring a large kettle of water to a boil and add one-half cup of baking soda; stir to dissolve. Add shells and bring back to boil. Boil rapidly three minutes. Drain and, with a small brush, remove any clinging particles from inside shell. Rinse thoroughly in very hot water, turn upside down on rack, and let dry completely. Shells may also be dried in a warm oven.

Alternatively, soak shells five minutes in hot water mixed with a little liquid detergent. Rinse several times and dry as above.

5. Preparing/Serving

As a rule of thumb, when planning to serve snails, allow three per person for an appetizer, soup or salad, and six to eight per person for a main dish. Snails have a delicate, slightly "woodsy" taste that can be appreciated without further embellishment. Nevertheless, snail meat is very "friendly" to a variety of flavors, so it can add interest, texture, and food value to the modern menu.

As with any delicate protein, such as egg-white, care must be taken not to overcook snail meat. And, an important caution: except for reheating, avoid the use of a microwave oven in preparing snails.

Most gourmet recipes using snail meat include the use of wine. Although most of the alcohol in the wine is cooked off in the process, some cooks would prefer not to use it. There are flavorful, non-alcoholic grape and apple juices available. The sweetness in these can be reduced by the addition of some unseasoned rice vinegar when the recipe calls for "dry" wine.

Snails parboiled and shelled

Appetizers

Snail Tempura

Escargot a la Bourguignonne

Snails in garlic butter, served with French bread for dipping into the delicious butter, are a familiar menu item. Here is the basic way to prepare these snails. Try some of the alternative seasonings. If there is any snail butter left over, refrigerate for making garlic bread on another occasion.

If you are serving the snails in their shells, you will need to provide tongs as well as small forks.

serves four

1 cup chicken or beef broth
1 cup dry white or red wine
2 tablespoons minced shallots
1 large clove garlic, minced
1 bay leaf
4 allspice berries, lightly crushed
24 fresh snails, parboiled, shelled and drained
garlic butter (recipe follows)
24 empty snail shells, or 4 escargot plates
3 tablespoons (approximately) very finely shredded Gruyère
 cheese
3-4 tablespoons fine dry breadcrumbs

In a saucepan or skillet, bring broth, wine, shallots, garlic, bay leaf and allspice berries to a boil. Lower heat slightly and let liquid reduce to approximately 1 1/2 cups. Add snails, bring back to boil and cook gently 10 minutes. Strain, reserving broth, and set snails aside.

Stuff each empty shell with approximately 3/4 teaspoon butter. Place snail meat into the shell and, if desired, sprinkle with a little cheese. Seal shell opening with a thick coating of garlic butter and dip into bread crumbs to cover lightly but completely.

Preheat oven to 450°. In a shallow baking pan, large enough to hold snails without crowding, heat 1/4 cup of the reserved snail liquid. Arrange snails in pan and bake in preheated oven 7 minutes. Broil 1 minute, or until crumbs are browned.

Alternatively, put 3/4 teaspoon butter in the recesses of the escargot plates and proceed as directed.

Garlic Butter
1/2 pound butter, at room temperature
1/2 cup minced fresh parsley
2 tablespoons very finely minced green onion tops
2 shallots, very finely minced
2 or 3 large cloves garlic, very finely minced
*1/8 teaspoon **each** salt and freshly ground white pepper*

Cream butter and combine with remaining ingredients until thoroughly blended.

Variations

Add to garlic butter:
Pinch powdered saffron, or to taste
1/4 teaspoon curry powder, or to taste
1/4 teaspoon ground cumin, or to taste
1 teaspoon fresh lemon juice and 1/4 teaspoon freshly grated
    lemon peel
1/4 teaspoon anchovy paste, or to taste
1 tablespoon minced fresh herbs, such as basil, savory,
    thyme, oregano
1 to 2 tablespoons ground walnuts or almonds.

Escargot ready for bread crumbs and the oven

13

Poppers

Ralph Tucker says that smaller snails may be used in this recipe, but to be sure they are at least six months old. (As with members of other species, all snails do not attain maximum size, regardless of age.) Any remaining marinara sauce may be heated and passed as a dipping sauce. The batter may be prepared a day in advance and stored, covered, in the refrigerator. Bon Appétit.

serves four to six

Batter:
1 egg
1 cup water
1 1/4 cups sifted all-purpose flour

In a bowl, beat egg and water until well mixed. Add all flour at once; beat until smooth. Cover and let stand at least 1 hour.

1 tablespoon olive oil
1 1/2 cups homemade or bottled marinara sauce
24 fresh snails, parboiled, shelled and drained
Peanut or canola oil for deep frying

Heat a 10 inch sauté pan and add olive oil, marinara sauce and the snails. Simmer over low heat until mixture thickens, about 10 minutes. Remove from heat.

Heat oil to 375°. Transfer half the batter to another bowl. Lift one snail at a time from marinara sauce, allowing a little sauce to cling, and dip into first bowl of batter. Deep fry until golden brown, remove, pat dry with paper toweling and dip into second bowl. Repeat deep frying. Drain on paper toweling; serve immediately.

Sautéed Escargot E'lite

Serve this simple snail rendition immediately after browning, either plain or with Salsa or Scampi Sauce. Recipes are given below.

serves four

12 fresh snails,parboiled, shelled and drained
Italian style bread crumbs
Butter

Dredge snails in Italian style bread crumbs. If you use Progresso, you can add more garlic powder and onion powder for added flavor. Sauté in butter until slightly golden.

Salsa (very hot)
3 ripe tomatoes, peeled and chopped
Juice of 1 lemon
1 small red onion, chopped
12 jalapeño peppers, seeded and minced
Salt and freshly ground black pepper to taste
1 tablespoon red wine vinegar (optional)
2 tablespoons vegetable oil (optional)

Combine tomatoes, lemon juice, onion, peppers, and salt and pepper. If a thinner salsa is preferred, add vinegar and oil. Mix well and chill.

Scampi Sauce

2 tablespoons plus 2 teaspoons vegetable oil
1/2 teaspoon freshly ground black pepper
2 tablespoons plus 2 teaspoons grated Parmesan cheese
1 tablespoon dried parsley flakes
1/8 teaspoon garlic powder
1/4 teaspoon salt
1 teaspoon crumbled dried oregano
1 tablespoon Worcestershire sauce
1/4 cup dry white wine

Combine all ingredients and heat almost to a boil.

Sautéed Snails and Almonds

Jeanne Jones, well-known cookbook author and columnist for King Features Syndicate, Inc., developed this recipe for those who do not like garlic. We have her permission to print it.

serves four

4 cups fresh spinach, stems removed, julienne cut
2 tablespoons corn-oil margarine
1/8 teaspoon salt
1/4 teaspoon freshly ground black pepper
12 canned snails, rinsed, drained
1/4 cup chopped almonds
*1/2 teaspoon **each**: Dijon mustard, extra virgin olive oil*
4 teaspoons balsamic vinegar
*1/4 cup **each**: light sour cream, water*

Arrange 1 cup spinach in a circle on each of 4 plates, making a hole, or nest, in the center.

Heat margarine, salt and pepper in a skillet and cook snails and almonds until lightly browned. Drain and put 3 snails and 1 table-spoon almonds in center of each spinach nest.

Combine mustard, oil and vinegar in another pan and reduce by 1/2 over medium heat. Add sour cream and water and blend until well-mixed. Spoon 2 tablespoons of sauce over top of each serving.

Preparation time: 20 minutes; cooking time: 10 minutes

Nutrition information, per serving:
140 calories; 18 mgs. cholesterol; 11 gms. fat; 186 gms. sodium.

Snail Fritters

serves eight

1 can (8 3/4 ounce) whole kernel corn
Milk as needed
1 egg, lightly beaten
1 1/2 cups sifted all purpose flour, or as needed
2 teaspoons baking powder
Peanut or canola oil for deep frying
24 fresh snails, parboiled, shelled and drained
Paper toweling
Sour cream or cream cheese

Drain liquid from corn into a measuring cup. Set corn aside and add milk to corn liquid to measure 1 cup. Combine with corn and egg. Sift together flour and baking powder, and stir into corn mixture; mix just until dry ingredients are moistened, adding additional flour if needed to make a stiff batter.

Preheat oil to 375°. Pat the snails dry with paper toweling. Press corn mixture around each snail to enclose completely and drop into hot oil. Do not overcrowd. Fry until golden brown, about 3 to 4 minutes. Remove snails from oil and drain on paper toweling. Serve with sour cream or cream cheese. Makes 2 dozen.

Snail Fritters with Tomato Sauce
Bigne di lumache con salsa di pomodoro a la Ralph Tucker

This recipe will serve a crowd. Be sure to use a large deep fryer, or several fryers, and bring oil back to temperature before each batch of snails is cooked. Provide napkins, small plates and forks.

2 quarts water
1/2 cup fresh lemon juice
3 sprigs parsley
6 dozen large fresh snails, parboiled, shelled and drained

Marinade
1 cup extra virgin olive oil
1/4 cup fresh lemon juice
2 tablespoons chopped fresh parsley
1 teaspoon salt
1/4 teaspoon freshly ground black pepper

Batter
1 egg, lightly beaten
1 cup ice water
2 tablespoons extra virgin olive oil
1 cup sifted all-purpose flour
*1/2 teaspoon **each** granulated sugar and salt*

Peanut oil or canola oil for deep frying
12 sprigs parsley, deep fried
3 lemons, quartered
3 cups tomato sauce, heated

Bring water, lemon juice, parsley and snails to a boil, lower heat and boil gently 10 minutes. While snails are cooking, combine marinade ingredients. Drain snails and place in nonmetallic bowl. Pour marinade over and let stand 1 hour.

Preheat peanut oil to 375°. Beat together egg, ice water, olive oil, flour, sugar and salt until dry ingredients are just moistened. Drain snails and pat dry with paper toweling.

Dip each snail in fritter batter and deep fry, without crowding, until golden brown. Remove and drain on paper toweling. Keep warn while frying remaining snails.

Arrange snail fritters on a heated serving platter and garnish with fried parsley and lemon wedges. Serve tomato sauce on the side.

Cassolettes D'Escargots

Incense of snails by Ralph Tucker

serves six

1/4 cup butter
2 cloves garlic, chopped
2 shallots, chopped
2 tablespoons chopped fresh parsley
1 pound small button mushrooms, trimmed
36 fresh snails, parboiled, shelled and drained
1 cup Riesling wine
1 cup heavy cream
1 tablespoon flour
Salt and pepper
Freshly ground nutmeg
12 slices French baguette, toasted

In a large saucepan, heat butter and sauté garlic, shallots, parsley and mushrooms for 5 minutes. Stir in snails and wine. Cover and simmer for 10 minutes. Mix cream and flour until smooth, pour into saucepan, stir and simmer until thickened. Season to taste with salt, pepper and nutmeg.

　　Place slices of baguettes on 6 individual plates. Spoon snails and sauce over top. Serve at once.

Snails Nestled in Zucchini Rounds

Select firm zucchini, one and one-half to two inches in diameter, enough for twelve slices, one and one-half inches thick. Prepare enough batter to make approximately one cup.

serves four

12 slices zucchini
Tempura batter mix
Peanut or canola oil for deep frying
4 tablespoons butter
1 large clove garlic, minced
12 large fresh snails, parboiled, shelled, and drained
1/2 cup shredded Mozzarella cheese

Prepare batter and set aside. Preheat oil to 375°. Make a hollow in each zucchini slice large enough to easily contain one snail. Dip slices in batter and deep fry just until slices are tender and golden brown. Remove and drain on paper toweling.

Preheat oven to 400°. In a skillet, melt butter and sauté garlic and snails for 10 minutes. Place one snail in each zucchini shell with a bit of butter and garlic sauce. Sprinkle top of each filled shell with cheese. Heat in oven until the cheese is melted.

Serve as *finger food*.

Snails in Tomato Sauce on Eggplant

Allow only two of these rich morsels per person unless the menu to follow is very light.

serves six

1 medium onion, chopped
2 cloves garlic, minced
1/2 cup chopped bell pepper
3 tablespoons virgin olive oil
1 can (8 ounce) tomatoes
Salt and freshly ground black pepper to taste
12 large fresh snails, parboiled, shelled and drained
2 small young eggplants
3/4 cups shredded Mozzarella cheese

Sauté onion, garlic, and bell pepper in 2 tablespoons of the oil until onion is translucent. Add tomatoes, salt and pepper; simmer until bell pepper is tender and flavors are blended. Add snails and simmer 10 minutes.

Place broiler rack at least 6 inches from heat source and preheat. Trim ends of eggplant and cut into twelve 1/2 inch slices. Brush slices on both sides with remaining oil and arrange on a baking sheet. Broil 5 minutes, or until eggplant is just tender. Preheat oven to 400°. Top each eggplant slice with a snail and spoon tomato sauce over. Sprinkle with cheese and bake 5 minutes, or until cheese is melted.

Snails in Pastry Shells

serves four

Marinade
1/4 cup white port wine
2 tablespoons wine vinegar
1 small onion, minced (about 1/4 cup)
1 clove garlic, minced
1 tablespoon soy sauce
1 teaspoon White Wine Worchestershire sauce
Freshly ground black pepper to taste
1/4 teaspoon ground cloves
Pinch of dried thyme

12 fresh snails, parboiled, shelled and drained

Pastry cups
1 1/2 cups sifted all-purpose flour
1/2 teaspoon salt
1/2 cup shortening
*4 tablespoons cold water, combined with 1 tablespoon
    white wine*

3/4 cup your favorite mushroom sauce

1/4 cup minced fresh parsley
1/4 cup freshly grated Parmesan cheese

Prepare the marinade by mixing together the marinade ingredients. Put the snails in a jar and add the marinade. Refrigerate 10 hours or overnight, shaking a few times to ensure that snails are covered with the marinade.

Sift flour and salt together; cut in shortening with pastry blender until pieces are the size of small peas. Sprinkle one tablespoon of the water mixture over part of it. Gently toss with fork. Push the dampened portion to the side of the bowl and repeat until all is dampened. Then lightly form the dough into a ball. For twelve pastry cups, divide the ball in half and wrap one piece in wax paper and refrigerate or freeze for later use. Flatten the other half on lightly floured surface by pressing with edge of hand three times across in both directions. Roll from center to edge until dough is 1/8 inch thick.

Preheat oven to 450°. Cut the dough into 3 inch circles (a wide-mouth fruit jar or ring makes a good cutter). Using a small size-

cupcake tin, press a dough circle over the bottom of each cup, pinching the dough to flute it. Prick entire surface with a fork. Bake in preheated oven for 10 to 12 minutes. When golden brown, turn out on wire rack to cool.

While the pastry shells are baking, transfer the snails and marinade to a sauce pan and simmer 10 minutes. Lift the snails from the marinade and place one in each of the baked shells.

Add the mushroom sauce to the marinade, cooking and stirring until well blended. Fill the shells with the sauce and sprinkle the tops lightly with minced parsley and grated Parmesan cheese.

Serve immediately.

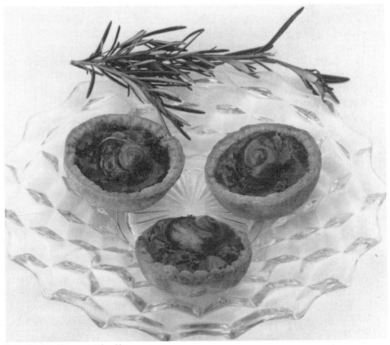

Snails in Pastry Shells

Ralph Tucker's Own Snail Recipe

serves four

1 tablespoon unsalted butter
3 tablespoons olive oil
1 tablespoon crushed garlic
1/4 cup dry white wine
24 fresh snails, parboiled, shelled, and drained
1/2 cup all purpose flour
1 teaspoon mixed chopped fresh herbs, such as basil,
  oregano, thyme, savory and sage

In a skillet, heat butter and 2 tablespoons of the oil. Add garlic, stir and add snails. Sauté snails until just tender and add wine. Cook, stirring, until wine is slightly reduced and thickened.
  Combine flour and herbs. In another skillet, heat remaining 1 tablespoon oil. Remove snails from sauté pan and dust with flour mixture. Over medium-high heat, sauté coated snails in oil until crisp, approximately 3 minutes.

Snail Tempura

serves eight

24 fresh snails, parboiled, shelled and drained
1 package tempura batter
Peanut or canola oil for deep frying

Prepare a batter according to your favorite recipe or packaged batter mix. Heat oil to 375°. Blot snails dry with paper toweling, and insert a round tooth pick into each. Dip each snail in batter to coat completely and drop into preheated oil. Do not overcrowd. Cook until lightly brown, remove from oil and drain on paper toweling. Serve with light white wine.

Escargot Marin

serves six

1/2 teaspoon **each** of fine herbs, celery salt, lemon zest (grated
   lemon rind) and paprika
1/4 cup flour
36 canned Petit Gris snails, drained
Peanut or canola oil for deep frying
Parsley and lemon wedges for garnish

Mix flour and herbs in a plastic bag. Preheat oil to 375°. Pat the
snails dry on paper toweling. Place them in the bag and shake until
covered with the flour mixture. Deep fry until lightly brown.
   Drain on paper toweling and garnish with parsley and lemon
wedges.

Snails with Leeks in Puff Pastry

serves six

1 sheet frozen puff pastry dough, thawed in refrigerator
6 fresh leeks, white part only
18 fresh snails, parboiled, shelled and drained
3 tablespoons butter
1 cup whipping cream
Parsley for garnish

Preheat oven to 375°. Divide pastry into three strips and arrange on
ungreased cookie sheet. Bake 18 minutes until puffed and slightly
browned. With a very sharp knife, cut each strip crossways through
the middle to make six pastries. Slit each strip to form a top and
bottom.
   Cut the leeks into 1/4 inch slices. Sauté with the snails in the butter
over moderate heat, shaking from time to time to cook evenly, but
do not brown. Add the whipping cream and stir gently. Let the
cream reduce on low heat while the puffs are browning.
   Put each pastry puff on a separate plate and top with 3 snails and
their sauce. Cover with a pastry top. Garnish plates with parsley.

Escargot Mendocino

serves eight

3 large shallots
1 cup California Pinot Noir
1 cup beef or chicken stock
36 canned Petit Gris snails, drained
2 tablespoons all purpose flour
Salt and freshly ground pepper to taste
36 crackers or toast points

Dice shallots and simmer in wine until reduced to about half. Add stock and snails and simmer 10 minutes. In a small dry skillet, brown the flour over medium heat, stirring frequently. Add to snail mixture to thicken the sauce. Salt and pepper to taste. Spoon onto crackers or toast points.

Napa Valley Escargot

serves six

3 large cloves garlic, minced
1/4 pound butter
1/4 cup chopped parsley
1/4 teaspoon freshly grated nutmeg
1/4 cup chopped shallots
1/8 teaspoon salt
36 canned Petit Gris snails, drained
Fresh baguette slices

Sauté together all ingredients except the snails and baguettes for 5 minutes, add drained snails and simmer over low heat 5 minutes. Place in individual serving dishes and serve with baguette slices.

Minnie's Breaded Snails

From Minnie Alvarado; this is Ralph Tucker's favorite snail recipe. It is especially good with Minnie's salsa recipe below.

serves five

1 clove garlic, minced
1/4 pound butter, melted
30 croutons, crushed with Italian seasonings
30 fresh snails, parboiled, shelled and drained

Sauté garlic in melted butter until golden brown. Shake the snails in the croutons until coated. Remove sautéed garlic from pan and add coated snails, sauté until golden brown.

Minnie's Salsa

3 ripe tomatoes
1 small red onion, chopped
Juice of 2 lemons,
One bunch cilantro
12 ounces or more (according to taste) jalapeño peppers
Salt to taste

Blanch tomatoes in boiling water. Remove the skin and chop tomatoes. Combine with onion and lemon juice. Let sit for about 10 minutes. Remove seeds from the jalapeños and chop finely. Add to tomato mixture. Salt to taste.

Snails with Country Ham and Garlic
a *la Ralph Tucker*

serves six to eight

2 tablespoons rendered pork fat or butter
2 tablespoons minced shallots
1 1/2 tablespoons minced prosciutto or Westphalian ham
1/2 cup dry white wine
1/2 cup rich meat or poultry stock
1 tablespoon minced garlic
1 teaspoon minced fresh thyme, or 1/4 teaspoon crumbled
  dried thyme
24 large fresh snails, parboiled, shelled and drained
1 medium tomato, peeled, seeded and cubed
1 tablespoon chopped fresh parsley
2 teaspoons anise liqueur
4 tablespoons unsalted butter at room temperature
Salt and freshly ground pepper

In large skillet heat fat over medium-low heat. Add shallots and ham and cook 5 minutes, stirring occasionally; do not brown. Tilt pan while pressing on shallots and ham with slotted spoon to drain off fat; blot fat with paper towel. Add wine, increase heat to medium high and cook until reduced to a glaze. Stir in stock, garlic and thyme. Blend well and add snails. Cover, reduce heat to low and simmer until thickened, about 10 minutes.

   Blend tomato, parsley and liqueur into sauce; cook until just heated. Do not allow sauce to boil or snails will toughen. Season with salt and pepper. Serve immediately.

Snail-Stuffed Mushroom Caps

serves four

1 pound large mushrooms, cleaned
1 tablespoon fresh lemon juice
1 quart water
2 dozen fresh snails, parboiled, shelled and drained
1 carton (8 ounce) whipped cream cheese with chives

Snap stems from mushrooms and rub a little lemon juice on each cap to prevent discoloration. Chop stems and add to water with remaining lemon juice, bring to boil, and add snails. Cook at gentle boil 10 minutes and drain.
   Preheat broiler. Place one snail in each mushroom cap, and cover with cream cheese. Broil 5 minutes, or until lightly browned.

Snail Ranch Snails

serves 30 to 35

100 snails parboiled, shelled and drained
1 lb butter
6-8 cloves of fresh garlic
1/4 teaspoon freshly grated nutmeg
1 teaspoon dill seed
1 bunch green onions
2 ounces dry Chablis
1/4 cup cracker meal
2 tablespoons minced fresh parsley
Baguettes

Melt butter. Mince garlic and green onions. Add garlic, green onions, nutmeg, dill and chablis to butter; blend well. Add cracker meal; blend. Add snails and simmer at least 10 minutes.
Serve with baguette bread rounds.

Snail Dolmas

Grape leaves are the traditional dolmas wrappings, but blanched Swiss chard or nasturtium leaves are also delicious treated in this way. Serve the dolmas as appetizers with plain yogurt, laced with lots of garlic, fresh lemon juice and chopped dill weed. Makes twenty-four dolmas.

serves six to eight

1/2 cup minced green onions and tops
1 teaspoon minced garlic
1 to 2 tablespoons olive oil
12 large fresh snails, parboiled, shelled, drained and minced
1 cup cooked white or brown rice
1 cup cooked garbanzo beans, lightly mashed
3 tablespoons minced fresh parsley
1 tablespoon **each** minced fresh oregano and basil
1/2 teaspoon salt
1/4 teaspoon freshly ground pepper
3 tablespoons fresh lemon juice
1 cup finely chopped ripe tomatoes
1 small jar grape leaves
1 1/2 cups consommé or beef broth

Sauté onions and garlic in oil 2 to 3 minutes. Add snails, rice, garbanzo beans, herbs, salt and pepper. Cook, covered, 3 minutes. Uncover and add 1 tablespoon of the lemon juice and the tomatoes. Raise heat and cook quickly until almost all moisture from tomatoes is absorbed. Adjust seasonings and set aside.

Cut tough stems from grape leaves, rinse in cold water, pat dry and place on work surface shiny side down. Put about 1 1/2 tablespoons filling on stem end of each grape leaf and roll up jelly roll fashion, folding sides in as you roll. Place rolls, in one layer, seam side down, in heavy shallow saucepan or skillet. Combine consommé with remaining 2 tablespoons lemon juice and add to saucepan. Place a plate on top of rolls to weigh down and bring consommé to gentle boil. Lower heat and simmer 15 to 20 minutes, depending upon size of rolls. Remove rolls to wire rack and cool. Serve at room temperature.

Variation
Substitute 2 cups cooked wild rice for the rice and garbanzo beans.

Escargots Carmel-by-the-Sea

Edward and Sue Borg serve this wonderful escargots with a glass of wine and fresh, crusty French bread. A glass of wine, a loaf of bread and Escargots Carmel-by-the-Sea — and thou!
The snails may be readied ahead of time and refrigerated. Bring to room temperature before serving.

serves four

1 1/2 cubes butter, at room temperature
2 large cloves garlic, finely minced
2 large shallots, finely minced
3 tablespoons chopped fresh parsley
Several gratings nutmeg
Salt and freshly ground pepper to taste
1/2 ounce dry white wine
1 dozen canned snails, rinsed and dried, or fresh snails,
    parboiled, shelled and drained
1 dozen snail shells

Cream butter and thoroughly blend in garlic, shallots, parsley, seasonings and wine.
    Preheat oven to 300°. With the handle of a teaspoon, stuff a small portion of the butter mixture into a shell. Insert a snail and cover snail with additional butter mixture. Repeat with remaining shells and snails.
    Place filled shells on baking sheet and bake in preheated oven 20 minutes.

Baked Snails

Serve these breaded snails right from their baking dish, or arrange on romaine lettuce leaves and let guests help themselves with toothpicks. If desired, offer your favorite yogurt/mint dipping sauce.

serves four

12 fresh snails, parboiled, shelled and drained
1/2 cup chopped onion
2 cloves garlic, chopped
2 whole allspice berries, lightly crushed
2 tablespoons fresh lemon juice
1 teaspoon freshly grated lemon peel
*1 tablespoon **each** melted butter and olive oil*
2/3 cup fine dry bread crumbs, tossed with
    1/2 teaspoon garlic salt
    1/8 teaspoon freshly ground white pepper
    1/8 teaspoon paprika
Romaine lettuce leaves (optional)
Lemon wedges
Mint sprigs

Place snails in a saucepan and add onion, garlic, allspice, lemon juice and lemon peel. Add water just to cover, bring to a boil, lower heat and simmer 10 minutes. Remove snails from cooking liquid and reserve liquid for another use.

Oil or butter a shallow baking dish large enough to hold snails without crowding. Preheat oven to 450°. Coat snails with butter and oil mixture and roll in bread crumb mixture, encasing completely. Bake in preheated oven 10 minutes, or until golden brown.

Arrange on lettuce leaves and garnish with lemon wedges and mint sprigs.

Soups

Onion Soup with Snails and Endive

Escargot Au Champagne

To enhance the flavor of this elegant soup, and to give it a pretty glaze, sprinkle with ground turmeric while sautéing. The delicate lavender color of the society chive blossoms add an intriguing touch. Serve as a first course soup.

serves six

2 dozen fresh snails, parboiled, shelled and drained
2 ounces smoked bacon, diced
1 clove garlic, minced
1 small onion, minced
*Pinch **each** crumbled bay leaf and crumbled dried thyme*
1 tablespoon olive oil
8 ounces champagne
Salt and freshly ground white pepper to taste
6 society chive blossoms

In a saucepan, over high heat, sauté snails, bacon, garlic, onion, bay leaf and thyme in olive oil 10 minutes, shaking pan gently from time to time. Season with salt and pepper and add champagne. Bring just to boil and ladle into warmed soup bowls. Garnish with blossoms and serve immediately.

Black Bean Soup with Snails

Serve this highly seasoned black bean soup as a main meal with freshly steamed white or brown rice. Be sure to pass a peppermill and a bottle of hot pepper sauce.

serves four

1/2 pound dried black beans, washed, soaked overnight in
    water to cover, and drained
5 cups beef or chicken stock
1/2 cup **each** minced onion, green or red bell pepper, minced
    celery and leaves, minced carrots
3 tablespoons olive oil
3 large cloves garlic, minced
1/2 teaspoon ground cumin, or to taste
1/2 tablespoon white vinegar
1/2 teaspoon Maggi's seasoning, or to taste
16 to 20 fresh snails, parboiled, shelled and drained
1 to 1 1/2 cups cubed cooked ham
Salt and freshly ground black pepper to taste
Cayenne pepper to taste
2 to 3 ounces mild goat cheese, crumbled or cut in small bits
Minced fresh parsley
Freshly steamed rice

In a large saucepan, combine drained beans and stock. Bring to a gentle boil, lower heat, cover with tilted lid and simmer 1 1/4 hours, or until beans are tender. Do not allow beans to get mushy.

While beans are cooking, in a large skillet, sauté onion, bell pepper, celery and carrots in oil until onions are lightly browned. Add garlic, cumin, vinegar and Maggi's seasoning. Mix well and toss in snails. Cook and stir over medium heat 5 minutes. With tongs, remove snails and set aside.

Drain a little water from the beans and add to vegetables. Cover and cook slowly approximately 30 minutes. When beans are tender, add vegetable mixture, reserved snails and ham, adding more stock if needed to make soup consistency. Season with salt, black pepper and cayenne; adjust seasonings with additional cumin, vinegar, and/or Maggi's seasoning. Heat until soup is piping hot.

Ladle soup into large, warmed bowls, being sure ingredients are divided evenly. Strew cheese over each filled bowl and sprinkle with minced parsley. Serve with small bowls of rice on the side.

Onion Soup with Snails and Endive

A quick, simple soup to tantalize your guests and introduce them to the joy of eating snails.

serves four

3 medium sized sweet onions, minced
1 tablespoon olive oil
4 cups chicken broth
1/2 cup dry white wine
12 fresh snails, parboiled, shelled and drained
1/2 teaspoon White Wine Worcestershire sauce
Salt and freshly ground black pepper to taste
12 leaves Belgium endive
1/4 cup freshly grated Parmesan cheese

Sauté onions in oil until translucent. In a saucepan, bring stock and wine to a gentle boil. Add onions, snails and Worcestershire sauce. Season with salt and pepper and simmer 10 minutes.

Place three endive leaves in each warmed soup bowl and ladle soup over, making sure each bowl contains 3 snails. Sprinkle with cheese and serve immediately.

Bisque of Snail and Artichoke

Ralph Tucker says that artichokes and snails complement each other. Try his bisque and see for yourself.

serves six to eight

48 fresh snails, parboiled, shelled and drained
2 tablespoons minced shallots
1 cup dry white wine
4 tablespoons unsalted butter
4 large artichoke hearts, cooked and chopped
2 1/2 cups sliced red onion
1 teaspoon minced garlic
1 teaspoon minced fresh oregano, or 1/4 teaspoon crumbled
  dried oregano
Dash cayenne pepper
2 tablespoons fresh lemon juice
3 cups fish stock or bottled clam juice
1 1/2 cups milk
1/2 cup heavy cream
1 to 2 ounces dry sherry
Salt and freshly ground white pepper to taste
Minced fresh chives
Paprika

In a saucepan or skillet, simmer snails and minced shallots in 3/4 cup of the wine 10 minutes. Remove from heat and set aside.

In a large saucepan, melt butter and sauté artichoke, onions and garlic until onions are translucent, sprinkling with oregano and cayenne pepper while cooking. Add lemon juice and cook 2 minutes, stirring well. Add fish stock, milk and remaining 1/4 cup wine; heat and simmer 2 minutes. Stir in cream and bring *just* to the boiling point. Immediately remove from heat and add snails and their wine.

In a blender or food processor, purée mixture until smooth. Return soup to saucepan and reheat without boiling. Add sherry and salt and pepper, reheat briefly and ladle into warmed soup bowls. Sprinkle with chives and dust with paprika. Serve immediately.

Shrimp and Snail Soup en Croûte

*Inspired by a recipe from French chef, Gilles Tournadre,
this "opulent potage" can be simplified by prior planning
and can be oven ready as early as eight hours ahead.
Serve it as the highlight of a grand luncheon with a salad
of mixed greens and a light dessert.*
    *Prepare your favorite fish stock up to two days ahead,
cover and refrigerate, or use bottled clam juice. Prepare
the stock base up to one day ahead.*

serves six

Stock Base
*1 pound large shrimp
2 tablespoons butter
1/2 cup chopped carrots
1/2 cup minced shallots
1/4 cup diced celery with some tops
2 sprigs parsley
1 sprig thyme
1 teaspoon freshly grated lemon peel
3 tablespoons brandy
2 cups dry white wine
10 cups fish stock
1 large bay leaf, crumbled
8 black peppercorns, lightly crushed
8 whole allspice berries, lightly crushed
8 whole coriander seeds, lightly crushed
1/2 teaspoon crumbled dried thyme*

For the Stock Base
Rinse shrimp, shell and de-vein; transfer shrimp to a bowl, cover
and refrigerate. In a food processor, chop shrimp shells; set aside.
In a large heavy skillet, melt butter and add carrot, shallots and
celery. Cover and cook over medium heat, stirring occasionally,
10 minutes, or until carrots have started to soften. Add parsley,
thyme, lemon peel and shells. Raise heat slightly and cook, stirring
to coat shells, 2 minutes. Pour brandy over and boil until liquid
has almost cooked away. Add 2/3 cup of the wine, reduce heat
and simmer until liquid is the consistency of syrup. In 2 additions,

repeat this procedure with remaining wine. Add 1 cup of the fish stock and simmer until liquid is reduced to a glaze. Repeat twice.

Add remaining 7 cups stock, bay leaf, peppercorns, allspice, coriander and thyme. Cover with tilted lid and simmer until liquid is reduced to 5 cups. Strain, using the back of a wooden spoon to press out as much liquid as possible. Cool, cover and refrigerate if not using immediately.

Soup
10 large cloves garlic, peeled
2 tablespoons butter
1 tablespoon light olive oil
1 cup minced onion
2/3 cup diced carrot
1/2 cup diced celery
1/4 cup minced fresh parsley
36 fresh snails, parboiled, shelled and drained
2 tablespoons minced fresh basil, or 2 teaspoons crumbled
    dried basil
1 tablespoon minced fresh savory, or 1 teaspoon crumbled
    dried savory
2 teaspoons minced fresh oregano, or 1/2 teaspoon
    crumbled dried oregano
reserved shrimp
1 bay leaf
1 can (1 pound) Italian tomatoes, drained and crushed
2 teaspoons brandy, or to taste
1 to 1 1/2 cups heavy cream
Salt and freshly ground white pepper to taste
4 ounces prosciutto, minced
2 sheets puff pastry
1 egg, lightly beaten

For the soup
Simmer garlic cloves in water to cover 10 minutes, or until tender. Drain and mash to a smooth paste; set aside.

In a large, heavy kettle, heat butter and oil over medium heat. Add onion, carrot, celery, parsley and snails; cook, stirring occasionally, 10 minutes. With tongs, remove snails and set aside. Add basil, savory, oregano and reserved shrimp to skillet and cook over high heat, stirring constantly, 1 minute just to partially cook shrimp. With tongs, remove shrimp and set aside. Add bay leaf and tomatoes to onion mixture and bring to boil. Stir in stock base and brandy and bring back to boil. Lower heat and simmer 5 minutes.

Snip reserved snails and shrimp into 1/2-inch pieces. Whisk reserved mashed garlic with a little of the cream and add to soup with remaining cream; season with salt and pepper and let cool.

Stir snails, shrimp and prosciutto into soup and ladle into six 2-cup, ovenproof soup bowls, making sure to divide the ingredients evenly.

On lightly floured surface, roll pastry 1/8 inch thick. Cut into rounds 2 inches larger than diameter of soup bowls. Brush rims of one side of pastry rounds with beaten egg, making an edging at least 1/2 inch wide. Without allowing pastry to touch the soup, place a round, egg side down, on top of each bowl. Stretch the round taut and press tightly against sides of bowl to seal completely. Brush tops of pastry with beaten egg and refrigerate at least 30 minutes, or up to 8 hours.

Remove soup bowls from refrigerator and place on a baking sheet; let stand at room temperature 30 minutes.

Preheat oven to 400°. Place baking sheet with soup bowls in oven. Bake 20 minutes, or until pastry is golden and puffed. Serve immediately.

Cream of Stilton and Onion Soup

Ralph Tucker has added snails to his favorite soup.

serves six to eight

4 tablespoons butter
36 fresh snails, parboiled, shelled and drained
1 pound onions, thinly sliced
1 or 2 large cloves garlic, minced
3/4 pound thick-skinned potatoes, peeled and cubed
1 quart lowfat milk
4 ounces Stilton cheese, crumbled
Salt and freshly ground white pepper to taste
Whipped cream (optional)
Minced fresh parsley

In a large, heavy saucepan, melt butter. When butter is hot, add snails; cook and stir 5 minutes. With slotted spoon, remove snails and set aside.

Add onions and garlic to butter, cover and cook over medium low heat, stirring occasionally, 15 minutes, or until onions are softened. Do not brown. Add potatoes and stir to coat completely with butter. Add milk, reduce heat, cover with tilted lid and simmer 30 minutes, or until potatoes are very soft.

Mince reserved snails finely and set aside. In a blender or food processor, purée soup in batches. Return soup to saucepan and add reserved minced snails and cheese. Stir over low heat until snails are heated and cheese is melted. Season with salt and pepper and ladle soup into warmed soup bowls. Garnish with whirls of whipped cream and sprinkle with minced parsley.

Corn and Snail Chowder *a la the Tuckers*

"My mother was an expert at cooking. The way she took corn off the cob was wonderful to watch. Her knives were sharp as razors and she was not timid. How could she be? She raised eight kids all by herself. But, back to the corn. Pick about six nice sized ears. Back in Nebraska, we used field corn and did not care whose field . . . Mom stood her ears on end and whoosh . . . off came the kernels and then she deftly turned the knife to scrape the milk and what was left. About now . . . start good sized snails sautéing . . . you know, wine, good oil, shallots and some fresh garlic."

serves four to six

36 fresh snails, parboiled, shelled and drained
1/2 cup dry white wine
1 teaspoon minced garlic
I small bay leaf
1/2 teaspoon crumbled dried oregano
8 green onions
1/2 cup grated onion
1/4 cup minced shallots
2 tablespoons unsalted butter
4 1/2 cups milk
1/4 teaspoon freshly ground white pepper
4 cups corn kernels with their milk
Salt to taste
Paprika

In a heavy skillet, bring snails, wine, garlic, bay leaf and oregano to a boil. Lower heat and cook, stirring, 10 minutes. Remove from heat, discard bay leaf and set aside.

Slice white of green onions and set tops aside. In a heavy saucepan, sauté green onion, grated onion and shallots in butter, stirring occasionally, 5 minutes, or until green onion is softened. Chop enough green onion tops to measure 1/3 cup; set aside. Add milk and pepper to onion mixture and bring to a boil . Add corn, stir quickly, heat and simmer 5 minutes, or until corn is just cooked. Add reserved snails and wine mixture, season with salt and heat through. Ladle into warmed soup bowls, sprinkle with reserved green onion tops and dust with paprika.

Brennan's Escargot and Wild Mushroom Soup

Ralph Tucker's adaptation of a recipe from the famous New Orleans restaurant. As did Gilles Tournadre, the chef at Brennan's tops his soup with puff pastry.

serves eight

6 ounces butter
48 fresh snails, parboiled, shelled and drained
20 fresh wild mushrooms, minced
1 tablespoon minced garlic
3 tablespoons minced shallots
3 quarts brown chicken stock
1/2 cup Pernod
1/4 cup reduced veal stock
1 quart heavy or half-and-half cream
2 tablespoons minced fresh basil, or 2 teaspoons crumbled dried basil
2 teaspoons minced fresh thyme, or 1/2 teaspoon crumbled dried thyme
Salt and freshly ground white pepper to taste
2 sheets puff pastry

In a large heavy saucepan, heat butter. Add snails and cook and stir over medium heat 5 minutes. Add garlic, shallots, and half of the minced mushrooms. Cook and stir 5 minutes. With tongs, remove snails and set aside.

Add stock and Pernod to saucepan. Bring to boil, add veal stock and cream, and cook at gentle simmer until soup is reduced to approximately 1 1/2 quarts. Add basil, thyme, and remaining mushrooms. Bring just to a boil and add reserved snails. Season with salt and pepper and ladle into 8 ovenproof soup cups.

On lightly floured board, roll pastry 1/8 inch thick. Cut into rounds 2 inches larger than diameter of the soup bowls. Being careful not to let rounds touch soup, fit a round on each bowl, stretch taut, and press against sides of bowl to seal completely. Refrigerate at least 30 minutes, or up to 8 hours. Remove from refrigerator, place on a heavy baking sheet and let stand at room temperature 30 minutes. Preheat oven to 400°. Bake soup 20 minutes, or until pastry is golden and puffed. Serve immediately.

Entrées

Snail Quiche

Snails Potted with Chopped Chicken Breasts

The origin of this interesting recipe is unknown. Serve as a luncheon entrée with French bread and fresh fruit salad. Note that it must be made the day before serving.

serves four to six

24 large fresh snails, parboiled, shelled and drained
1 tablespoon minced shallots
1 tablespoon minced garlic
2 tablespoons unsalted butter
1/2 cup red Zinfandel wine
1 whole chicken breast, boned, skinned, and diced
1/4 cup heavy cream
1/2 teaspoon salt
1/4 teaspoon freshly ground white pepper
1/2 cup minced fresh parsley
1/4 cup dried French bread crumbs
1/4 pound bacon, blanched
Romaine or red lettuce leaves
Cherry tomatoes, halved
Cornichons
Watercress sprigs

Sauté snails, shallots and garlic in butter 2 to 3 minutes, or until shallots have softened. Add the wine and simmer, uncovered, until liquid is reduced by half, removing snails after 5 minutes. Quarter the snails and set aside. Strain and reserve the wine reduction.

In a food processor, purée chicken breasts and blend in cream, salt and pepper, wine reduction, parsley and reserved snails. Pulse 1 or 2 seconds and blend in bread crumbs to thoroughly blend. Do not overprocess.

Preheat oven to 350°. Line a terrine mold with bacon slices and spoon purée into mold, tapping mold several times against kitchen counter to compact the mixture. Cover with bacon, cover mold tightly and place in a deep pan. Add boiling water to come halfway up sides of mold and bake 40 to 45 minutes. Remove terrine from waterbath, cool and refrigerate overnight, or for up to 2 days.

Turn pâté out of terrine and cut into slices. Arrange lettuce leaves on serving plates and top with slices. Garnish with tomatoes, cornichons and watercress.

Escargot a la Penne

serves four

48 Petit Gris canned snails
*2 tablespoons **each** olive oil and butter*
1 teaspoon minced garlic
1 teaspoon minced fresh oregano, or 1/4 teaspoon crumbled
 dried oregano
1 cup heavy or half-and-half cream
1 package (10 1/2-ounce) frozen peas
1/2 cup minced water chestnuts
2/3 cup freshly grated Parmesan cheese
Salt and freshly ground black pepper to taste
*1/2 pound penne pasta, cooked **al dente***
Minced fresh basil or parsley

Drain snails. In a heavy skillet, heat oil and butter. Add snails, garlic
and oregano and sauté 3 minutes. Stir in cream and simmer until
mixture thickens slightly. Add peas, water chestnuts, half the cheese
and salt and pepper. Reheat, being careful not to overcook.

Drain penne and toss with escargot sauce until well coated.
Mound on heated serving platter and sprinkle with basil. Pass
remaining cheese.

Snail and Sweetbread Lasagne

A different way to serve lasagne. Work quickly when assembling, so the stacks do not dry out. Serve with crusty French bread and a spinach salad.

serves four

*1/2 pound veal sweetbreads
1 small onion, chopped
1 small carrot, chopped
1 rib celery and some tops, chopped
1 cup peeled, seeded and chopped tomatoes
1 bay leaf
8 black peppercorns, lightly crushed
2 cups water
1 cup dry white wine
24 large fresh snails, parboiled, shelled and drained
1 tablespoon **each** butter and olive oil
2 tablespoons heavy cream
Pinch anise seeds
Salt and freshly ground black pepper to taste
1/2 cup minced shallots
12 pieces (3 by 2 1/2 inches) flat green pasta, cooked **al dente**
    and drained
Béarnaise sauce (recipe follows)
1/4 cup freshly grated Parmesan cheese*

Soak sweetbreads in ice water 15 minutes. Drain and repeat with fresh water; let stand 15 minutes and drain. In a large saucepan, combine onion, carrot, celery, 1/2 cup of the tomatoes, bay leaf and peppercorns. Add water, wine and sweetbreads. Bring to a boil, lower heat, cover and cook at gentle boil 10 minutes. Add snails and cook an additional 10 minutes.

Strain mixture, reserving liquid. Trim fat and membrane from sweetbreads. Chop sweetbreads and snails coarsely and set aside.

In a saucepan, heat butter and oil. Add shallots and sauté until soft. Add reserved sweetbreads and snails, cream, anise seeds and salt and pepper to taste. Heat without boiling and keep warm, adding a little of the reserved sweetbread poaching liquid as needed to moisten.

Arrange 4 pasta squares on a heated serving plate. Cover each square with a layer of snail mixture, top with another square and repeat procedure, making 3 layers of pasta and 2 layers of filling. Cover loosely with aluminum foil and keep warm while making the Béarnaise sauce.

Spoon the sauce over each portion, sprinkle with cheese and garnish with remaining chopped tomatoes.

Béarnaise Sauce
2 egg yolks
1 tablespoon reserved sweetbread poaching liquid
2 or 3 drops hot pepper sauce
*1/8 teaspoon **each** paprika, salt, freshly ground white pepper*
1/4 pound butter, chilled
2 tablespoons minced fresh basil

In the top of a double broiler, with a whisk, beat together the egg yolks, poaching liquid and hot pepper sauce to blend well. Bring water in bottom of double boiler to a bare simmer. (Do not allow to boil at any time.) Set pan over simmering water. Add butter in thin squares, stirring constantly until butter has melted and the sauce is thickened. Adjust seasonings and stir in basil.

entrées

Snail and Mushroom Ramekins

*In this recipe, Ralph Tucker uses canned snails with great
results. For a special treat, before toasting the bread,
spread it with garlic butter. Garnish the plate on which
you put the ramekins with small clusters of seedless red
grapes.*

serves six

*2 large cloves garlic, minced
2 large shallots, minced
1 pound fresh button mushrooms, halved if necessary to make
  uniform in size
1 teaspoon minced fresh sage, or 1/4 teaspoon crumbled dried
  sage
2 tablespoons **each** olive oil and butter
36 large canned escargots, drained
1 cup dry white wine
1/2 tablespoon cornstarch
1 cup heavy or half-and-half cream
3 tablespoons minced fresh parsley
Salt and freshly ground white pepper to taste
Freshly grated nutmeg to taste
Minced fresh chives
Paprika
18 slices French baguette, toasted
Seedless red grape clusters*

In a large skillet, sauté garlic, shallots, mushrooms and sage 5 minutes in oil and butter. Add escargots and wine. Cover and simmer
5 minutes. Mix cornstarch with a little of the cream to make a thin
paste and blend into remaining cream. Stir into mushroom mixture
and cook, stirring often, 5 minutes, or until thickened. Stir in parsley
and season with salt and pepper and nutmeg.

Spoon escargots mixture into 6 heated ramekins and sprinkle with
chives and paprika. Tuck 3 slices of toast around edge of each dish
and serve immediately.

50

Parsley Pasta with Snails and Clams

You will thank whoever developed this recipe, for snails and clams do well together. All you need to accompany this dish is steamed broccoli, your favorite hard rolls and a bowl of freshly grated Parmesan cheese.

serves four to six

3 large cloves garlic, minced
1 large shallot, minced
1/4 cup olive oil
2 cans (15 ounce) whole baby clams
1 large ripe tomato, seeded and coarsely chopped
1/4 cup loosely packed chopped parsley
1/4 cup dry white wine
48 fresh snails, parboiled, shelled and drained
Salt and freshly ground black pepper to taste
*1 pound dried pasta of choice, cooked **al dente** and drained*
Minced fresh dill weed

In a large skillet, sauté garlic and shallot in oil 4 minutes, or until softened. Drain liquid from clams into skillet; set clams aside. Add tomato, parsley and wine to skillet, bring to a boil, lower heat and simmer 4 minutes, or until slightly thickened.

    Add clams and snails, reheat thoroughly and season with salt and pepper. Toss well with pasta and mound on heated serving platter. Sprinkle generously with dill and serve immediately.

Snails Nestled In New Potatoes

Adapted from a recipe by the former Gourmet Cuisine, Intl., these potato nests could be served as an appetizer or a main meal. Steam and fill the potatoes up to one day in advance. Refrigerate; bring to room temperature before baking.

The sauce must be made the last minute, but the reduction can be done ahead of time and all ingredients readied.

serves six

36 tiny (1½"–2") new red potatoes, scrubbed
2 cups dry white wine
2 teaspoons minced fresh tarragon, or 1/2 teaspoon crumbled dried tarragon
1 carrot, chopped
1 onion, chopped
1 rib celery, chopped
4 tablespoons minced shallots
4 black peppercorns, lightly crushed
Bouquet garni of bay leaf, oregano, parsley and thyme
72 Petit Gris snails
1 cup toasted fine white bread crumbs
3 tablespoons butter, at room temperature
1 large clove garlic, minced
1/8 teaspoon freshly ground black pepper
1 tablespoon brandy
Olive oil and butter for sautéing
Tarragon sauce (recipe follows)
Watercress sprigs

Steam potatoes, in batches if necessary, 4 minutes, or until they *just* start to soften. Immediately drop into cold water; when cool, cut bottoms so each potato stands flat. With a melon baller, cut a hollow in the center of each potato a little larger than a snail. Set aside.

In a saucepan, bring wine, tarragon, carrots, onion, celery, 2 table-spoons of the shallots, peppercorns and bouquet garni to a boil. Reduce heat slightly and cook 10 minutes. Add snails and simmer 5 minutes. Strain into a large sieve, reserving liquid. With tongs, remove snails and set aside.

With a fork, blend bread crumbs, 3 tablespoons butter, garlic, remaining 2 tablespoons shallots, ground pepper and brandy; set aside.

In a large skillet, sauté reserved potato boats in oil and butter until lightly browned. Preheat oven to 400°. Arrange potato nests on heavy baking sheets and tuck 2 snails into each hollow. Cover snails with a coating of the bread crumb mixture and bake 10 minutes, or until crumbs are browned.

Spoon tarragon sauce on 6 warmed plates and arrange 6 potato nests on the sauce. Garnish with watercress and serve immediately. Pass remaining sauce.

Tarragon Sauce
Reserved snail poaching liquid
Juice of 1/2 lemon
1/4 cup heavy cream
1 teaspoon fresh tarragon, or 1/2 teaspoon crumbled dried
 tarragon
7 tablespoons butter
Salt and freshly ground white pepper to taste
1 egg yolk

Over high heat, boil reserved poaching liquid until reduced to 1/2 cup. Add lemon juice, cream and tarragon and bring just to boil. Reduce heat and, bit by bit, whisk in butter. Season with salt and pepper and quickly incorporate egg yolk into the sauce. Remove from heat immediately.

Snail and Mushroom Rumaki

Have your barbecue fire ready. The grill should be approximately four inches above the hot coals.
  Serve the rumaki with cheese-flavored mashed potatoes and a green vegetable.

serves four

1/4 cup minced shallots
1/4 cup olive or canola oil
2 tablespoons fresh lemon juice
1/2 teaspoon salt
1/4 teaspoon freshly ground black pepper
1 tablespoon minced fresh parsley
24 large fresh snails, parboiled, shelled and drained
6 large slices lean bacon, blanched
20 medium to large fresh mushrooms, cleaned
Fresh lemon juice
Lemon wedges
Watercress or parsley sprigs

In a nonmetallic dish, combine shallots, oil, 2 tablespoons lemon juice, salt, pepper and parsley. Add snails and stir to coat. Tossing several times, marinate in refrigerator 4 hours. Drain snails and pat dry with paper toweling. Set aside.

  Cut each bacon slice into 4 strips. Snap stems from mushrooms and refrigerate for later use in soup stock. Rub caps with lemon juice to prevent discoloration.

  Wrapping each snail in a strip of bacon as you work, and starting and ending with a snail, alternately thread 6 snails and 4 mushroom caps on 4 thin skewers.

  Grill, turning several times, 5 minutes, or until bacon is crisp.

California Escargot Fettuccine

Serve the fettuccine with garlic bread, a tossed mixed green salad and a glass of chilled Chardonnay. Pass lots of grated cheese.

serves four

24 fresh snails, parboiled, shelled and drained
3 tablespoons butter
4 or 5 large cloves garlic, minced
1/2 teaspoon crumbled dried thyme
1/2 cup chicken broth
1/2 can (10 1/2-ounce) cream of mushroom soup
1/2 pound dried fettuccine, cooked **al dente**
Freshly grated Parmesan cheese
2 tablespoons **each** *minced fresh parsley and chives*

Snip snails in half. In a skillet, melt butter and add snails, garlic and thyme. Cook and stir over medium high heat 3 minutes. Add broth, bring to a gentle boil, lower heat and simmer 8 minutes. Stir in mushroom soup and blend well. Reheat and quickly toss with drained pasta. Transfer to heated serving platter. Sprinkle with cheese and herbs.

California Escargot Fettuccine

Snail and Beef Ragoût

For variety, serve this tasty stew on a bed of steamed millet instead of the usual rice. A tossed green salad will complete the meal.

serves four

24 fresh snails, parboiled, shelled and drained
1/4 cup fresh lemon juice
1 tablespoon canola oil
12 ounces beef tenderloin tips, cut into thin slivers
1 tablespoon chopped shallots
1 large clove garlic, minced
1 to 2 teaspoons drained green peppercorns
1/2 tablespoon flour
1 cup dry red wine
1 tablespoon minced fresh parsley
1 teaspoon minced fresh basil
Salt and freshly ground black pepper to taste
Steamed millet
Ripe tomato wedges

Place snails and lemon juice in a saucepan and add water to cover. Bring to a boil, lower heat and simmer 8 minutes. Drain, reserving broth. Set snails aside.

In a heavy skillet, heat oil until very hot. Add beef slivers, stirring with a fork, and quickly brown on all sides. With slotted spoon, remove beef to a bowl and set aside.

Add shallots and garlic to skillet and cook, stirring, until shallots just start to brown. Add reserved snails and peppercorns and sauté 2 minutes. Sprinkle with flour and stir well. Gradually add wine and 1/2 cup of the reserved snail broth. Bring to a gentle boil and cook, stirring, until thickened. Add parsley, basil and salt and pepper. Return beef to skillet and quickly reheat.

Mound steamed millet on heated serving platter and top with ragoût. Arrange tomato wedges around and serve immediately.

Snail and Beef Ragoût

Snail Quiche

A perfect treat for a special brunch. Serve this or the following quiches with a crisp green salad, sparkling white wine and a simple fruit dessert.

The pie crust may be made ahead and refrigerated or frozen; if frozen, defrost overnight in refrigerator.

To vary the pie crust, substitute dry white wine for the water and vinegar.

serves six to eight

Pie Crust
1 1/2 cups sifted all-purpose flour
1/2 teaspoon salt
1/2 cup shortening, chilled
4 tablespoons ice water, mixed with
1 tablespoon vinegar

Filling
2 large shallots, minced
36 large fresh snails, parboiled, shelled, drained and halved
2 tablespoons butter
1/4 teaspoon Fines Herbs
1/4 teaspoon freshly ground white pepper
1 large clove garlic, finely minced
2 tablespoons finely minced fresh parsley
1 tablespoon finely minced fresh chives
4 eggs
1 cup heavy or half-and-half cream
1/4 cup dry white wine
1/2 teaspoon salt
1/8 teaspoon freshly grated nutmeg
1/4 cup freshly grated Parmesan cheese
2/3 cup finely shredded Gruyère cheese
Paprika

For the Pie Crust:

Sift flour and salt together; with a pastry blender, cut in shortening until the consistency of coarse cornmeal. Sprinkle water and vinegar over and, with a fork, toss and mix until flour is moistened. Do not overmix. With hands, gently form into a ball, flatten ball into a round disc, wrap in waxed paper and refrigerate at least 1 hour, or overnight.

On a lightly floured board, press disc of dough to further flatten and, starting at center and working towards edges, roll dough into a round 1/8 inch thick. Transfer to a 10- inch pie pan and flute edges. Trim excess crust, cover with plastic wrap and refrigerate at least 30 minutes.

Preheat oven to 400°. Line the bottom of chilled pie shell with lightweight aluminum foil large enough so it hangs over sides of crust and can be easily lifted out. Fill the foil-lined shell with metal pie weights or with raw rice or legumes halfway up the sides of the shell. Crimp the foil so that it covers the exposed rim of the crust to prevent burning.

Bake the weighted shell in preheated oven 10 minutes. Remove from oven, lift out the foil and weights, prick the entire bottom surface of the shell with the tines of a fork and return the shell to the oven. Bake an additional 5 minutes, then remove from the oven, place on a wire rack and let cool completely before filling.

For the Filling:

In a skillet, sauté shallots and snails in butter 10 minutes, sprinkling with Fines Herbs and 1/8 teaspoon of the pepper while sautéing. Toss in garlic, parsley and chives and set aside to cool. In a bowl, beat eggs, cream, wine, salt, remaining 1/8 teaspoon pepper and nutmeg.

Preheat oven to 375°. Sprinkle prebaked crust with Parmesan cheese and fill with reserved snails. Pour egg mixture over and cover with Gruyère cheese. Sprinkle with paprika and bake 40 to 50 minutes, or until cake tester inserted in center of custard comes out clean.

Escargot Quiche Piper Johnson

Terry and Nicholas give their quiche a distinctive flavor by smoking the snails. Sometimes they add mesquite or hickory chips to the coals for added flavor. Terry advises that you can refrigerate a quiche for later reheating and serving but don't freeze a quiche. It will become soggy.

serves eight

Pastry Dough
6 ounces unsalted butter (room temperature)
1 teaspoon salt
2 eggs
1 tablespoon milk
2-2 1/2 cups all-purpose flour

Cream the butter and salt. Add the eggs and milk and mix for a few seconds. Add all the flour at one time and mix just until the pastry forms a ball. Chill at least 1 hour. Roll as directed in preceding quiche recipe.

Quiche
Pastry dough
1 egg yolk lightly beaten for egg wash

Filling for Quiche
1/4 cup finely chopped onions
36 fresh snails, parboiled, shelled and drained
1 tablespoon olive oil
1/2 cup (3 ounces) Gruyère cheese, grated
7 large eggs
3 cups heavy cream or 1/2 heavy cream and 1/2 milk
1/2 teaspoon freshly ground white pepper
3 large cloves garlic, minced

Preheat oven to 350°. Line a buttered 10 or 11 inch quiche pan with the pastry dough, but do not trim edges. Line the pastry with aluminum foil or parchment paper. Fill with aluminum beans (or dried beans) and bake for 20 minutes. Take from the oven and remove beans. Brush the bottom of the crust with beaten egg and return the quiche crust to oven for 10 minutes. Remove to rack and cool.

Meanwhile, smoke the snails. Place whole snails with the tablespoon of olive oil in a skillet on a hot grill with a cover. When cool, chop coarsely.

Sauté onions with chopped snails and crushed garlic 4 to 5 minutes. Preheat oven to 350°.

Sprinkle 1/4 cup of the cheese into baked shell. Add sauté mixture. In a large bowl, combine eggs with remaining ingredients until blended, pour into shell. Trim edges of shell. Top with remaining cheese. Bake in preheated oven for 50 minutes or until the quiche has puffed and browned. Cut into wedges and serve on warmed plates.

Spinach Snail Quiche

To make this colorful quiche, follow the directions in the recipe on page 58 for preparing and prebaking the pie crust.

serves six

1 9-inch prebaked pie shell
3 tablespoons freshly grated Parmesan cheese
1/2 package (10 1/2-ounce) frozen chopped spinach, thawed
36 snails, parboiled, shelled and drained
2 tablespoons olive oil
2 tablespoons dry white wine
2 tablespoons minced red onions
2 tablespoons minced red bell peppers
2 teaspoons minced fresh parsley
1 tablespoon dry sherry
4 eggs
1 3/4 cups heavy or half-and-half cream
1/2 teaspoon **each** *Fines Herbs and salt*
1/4 teaspoon freshly ground black pepper
1/2 cup shredded Gruyère cheese

Sprinkle prebaked crust with Parmesan cheese and refrigerate. Place the half package of spinach in a strainer and press out *all* moisture; set aside.

In a skillet, sauté snails in 1 tablespoon of the oil, covered, 5 minutes. Add wine and cook, stirring, until wine has evaporated. Remove from heat and set aside.

In another skillet, sauté onions and red peppers in remaining oil 2 minutes. Add spinach, stir well, cover and cook 3 minutes. Remove from heat and add parsley, sherry and reserved snails. Cool.

Preheat oven to 375°. In a bowl, beat eggs lightly with cream and seasonings. Combine with snail mixture and pour into prepared pie shell. Bake 40 to 50 minutes, or until quiche tests done.

Scalloped Snails and Tomatoes

A favorite recipe adapted from LEFTOVERS, by Coralie Castle.

serves two

2 tablespoons minced onion
2 tablespoons minced bell pepper
3 tablespoons butter
8 large snails, parboiled, shelled, drained
   and coarsely chopped
1 1/4 cups chopped ripe tomatoes
1/2 to 2/3 cup cooked corn kernels
2 tablespoons slivered ripe olives
1/2 teaspoon granulated sugar
1/4 teaspoon **each** salt and crumbled
   oregano or sage
1/8 teaspoon freshly ground black pepper
1/2 cup cubed stale bread
1/4 cup Parmesan Crumb Topping (recipe follows)

Preheat oven to 350° F. Sauté onion and bell pepper in 2 tablespoons of the butter until softened. Add snails and cook, stirring, 2 minutes. Combine with tomatoes, corn, olives, sugar, seasonings and bread. Adjust seasonings and transfer to shallow baking dish.

Sprinkle mixture evenly with crumb topping and dot with remaining 1 tablespoon butter. Bake in preheated oven 15 to 20 minutes, or until heated through and lightly browned.

Parmesan Crumb Topping
Toss 2 cups fresh bread crumbs with 3 tablespoons melted butter to coat evenly. Toss in 1/4 cup freshly grated Parmesan cheese. Store in jar with tight lid, refrigerated, for up to 1 week.

Snails with Wild Mushrooms and Tomato Basil Butter

From the well known restaurant, La Belle Helene, *for years a landmark of St. Helena, California, comes this elegant snail recipe. Fresh mushrooms, now available in many markets, make a world of difference. To accommodate those watching fat intake, the butter in the sauce has been reduced.*

serves three or four

4 ounces chanterelle mushrooms
4 ounces cèpe mushrooms
2 tablespoons unsalted butter
2 large shallots, minced
1 large clove garlic, pressed
1 sprig thyme
1 bay leaf
3 whole white peppercorns, lightly crushed
1 large ripe tomato, peeled, seeded and diced
1/2 teaspoon granulated sugar
1/4 teaspoon salt
1/2 cup dry white wine
1/2 cup heavy cream
6 to 8 basil leaves
1/4 pound salted butter, cut into bits
24 large, canned Burgundy snails
2 tablespoons Pernod liqueur, heated
Salt and freshly ground black pepper
Toast points
Parsley sprigs

Wash, dry and quarter mushrooms; set aside.

In a saucepan set over medium heat, melt 1 tablespoon of the unsalted butter. Add one of the minced shallots, garlic, thyme, bay leaf and peppercorns. Cook until shallot is translucent. Add tomato, sugar and salt; cook for 10 minutes.

Blend wine into tomato mixture and let boil until reduced by one-half. Add cream and bring just to a boil. Add basil, lower heat and reduce sauce at simmer for 5 minutes.

One piece at a time, whisk salted butter into tomato mixture, stirring until butter has melted. Purée mixture in blender until smooth, strain through fine sieve and set aside.

In a sauté pan set over high heat, melt remaining tablespoon unsalted butter. Stirring almost constantly, sauté mushrooms and remaining minced shallot 3 minutes. Reduce heat to medium and add snails. Simmer 5 minutes and season to taste with salt and pepper. Pour Pernod over and ignite, tossing pan until flames subside. Blend in tomato sauce, bring *just* to a boil and transfer to heated plates. Surround each serving with toast points and garnish with parsley.

Snails in Lettuce Leaves

Vary these paupiettes, _or rolls, by substituting blanched Savoy cabbage leaves for the lettuce leaves._

serves six

36 snails, parboiled, shelled and drained
1/2 cup olive oil
4 tablespoons minced shallots
1 cup chopped fresh mint
2/3 cup mashed cooked carrots
1/3 cup cooked rice creole
1/4 teaspoon **each** salt, freshly ground white pepper and
    ground mace
2 tablespoons butter, room temperature
6 large Boston lettuce leaves, lightly blanched
1 cup chicken stock

Sauce
1 1/2 teaspoons butter
1 1/2 teaspoons flour
1/2 cup heavy or half-and-half cream
Juice of 1/2 lemon
Mint or parsley sprigs

Place snails in glass or ceramic bowl with olive oil, 2 tablespoons of the shallots and 1/2 cup of the mint. Cover and marinate in refrigerator 24 hours, tossing occasionally.

Remove snails and strain marinade into a saucepan. Heat marinade, add snails and cook 3 minutes. With slotted spoon, remove snails and place in bowl with carrots, rice creole, remaining 2 tablespoons shallots and 1/4 cup of the remaining mint. Add salt, pepper and mace; blend in butter. Place lettuce leaves flat on work surface and divide snail mixture among them. Roll leaves like a jelly roll, folding in sides to form paupiettes. In one layer, place rolls seam side down in a skillet large enough to hold rolls snugly. Heat stock, pour over paupiettes, cover skillet, bring stock to gentle boil, lower heat and simmer 8 minutes, basting often.

Carefully remove paupiettes and arrange on heated platter; keep warm. Strain stock and set aside.

For the sauce
Melt butter and blend in flour; cook, stirring, 3 minutes. Combine reserved stock and heavy cream; gradually add to roux and cook, stirring constantly, until sauce thickens and comes *just* to a boil. Adjust seasonings and stir in lemon juice and remaining 1/4 cup of mint.
  Spoon sauce over paupiettes and surround with mint sprigs. Serve immediately.

Fresh Snails in Jumbo Pasta

From Mary Stewart at E'lite, comes this perfect luncheon dish, accompanied by a crisp green salad, or a dinner entrée after a first course of sautéed vegetable with vinaigrette. The recipe calls for sixteen instead of twelve pasta shells in case a few break during cooking.

serves two

3 cloves garlic, minced
1 green onion, minced
1/2 cup good white wine
2 tablespoons virgin olive oil
12 large, fresh snails, parboiled, shelled and drained
1 cup ricotta cheese
1 tablespoon freshly grated romano cheese
2 teaspoons minced parsley
1 pinch ground cinnamon
16 jumbo pasta shells
Cherry tomatoes, halved if large
Parsley or watercress sprigs

In a covered skillet, cook garlic and green onion in wine and oil until tender. Add snails and cook over low heat 10 minutes, stirring occasionally. Remove from heat and reserve. Combine ricotta cheese and remaining ingredients and set aside.
  Bring a large kettle of water to a boil and cook pasta shells until just *al dente*. Rinse in cold water. Carefully stuff 12 of the shells with the cheese mixture. Push a snail into each stuffed shell and place in skillet. Pour garlic/onion sauce over and quickly reheat. Transfer to heated serving plate and garnish with tomatoes and parsley.

Coho Salmon Stuffed with California Snails

George Francisco's elegant salmon stuffed with snails is a good example of the work of his kitchen in the Mount View Hotel in Calistoga, California. The grilled vegetables are best marinated overnight. The stuffing and sauce should be prepared shortly before braising the salmon.

serves four

For the Balsamic Marinade and Grilled Vegetables
1 tablespoon fresh lemon juice
2 tablespoons balsamic vinegar
4 tablespoons olive oil
Bit of garlic, herbs, salt and pepper
4 Japanese eggplants, halved lengthwise
2 leeks, white only, quartered lengthwise
2 zucchini, quartered lengthwise
1 head radicchio, broken
Olive oil for brushing vegetables

Thoroughly combine lemon juice, vinegar, olive oil, garlic, herbs and seasonings. Brush vegetables lightly with oil and grill until cooked halfway. Transfer hot vegetables to a bowl and pour marinade over. Cover with plastic wrap and refrigerate overnight.

For the Stuffing
4 tablespoons butter
1/2 teaspoon minced garlic
1 teaspoon minced fresh herbs of choice
24 fresh snails, parboiled, shelled and drained
1/4 cup freshly chopped morel mushrooms, or mushrooms of choice
1/4 cup white wine
Salt and freshly ground black pepper

Heat butter in a skillet and add garlic and herbs. Cook for a few seconds. Add snails and mushrooms; cook for 1 minute. Raise heat slightly and deglaze skillet with wine. Reduce until liquid has almost evaporated. Remove skillet from heat and season snail mixture with salt and pepper.

For the Black Pepper Sauce

*1/4 cup **each** fish stock and white wine*
6 tablespoons butter
2 teaspoons cracked black pepper
Salt to taste

In a saucepan bring stock and wine to boil and reduce until 1 tablespoon remains. Whisking constantly, stir in butter 1 tablespoon at a time; do not allow to boil. After all butter is incorporated, stir in pepper and salt. Keep warm.

For the Braised Stuffed Salmon

Four 8-ounce whole boneless and gutted Coho salmon
Salt and freshly ground black pepper
2 cups fish stock

Preheat oven to 350°.
    Pat salmon dry and lightly season inside with salt and pepper. Divide stuffing into 4 portions and stuff each fish with a portion. In a large ovenproof skillet, bring stock to a boil and carefully lower fish into boiling stock. Cover and place in preheated oven. Cook approximately 7 minutes, depending on size of fish. To check for doneness, open one of the fish and make sure it's just cooked through and the stuffing is hot.
    Place cooked fish on heated plates with the belly side facing you. Ladle the butter sauce on the belly side of the plate and top with any stuffing that has fallen out of the salmon. Arrange grilled vegetables decoratively on the other side of the fish.

Snail Stuffed Twice-Baked Potatoes

So easy because the potatoes may be stuffed in advance, this lowfat entree will please the entire family. If making ahead and refrigerating, let stand at room temperature one hour before reheating.

serves four

12 large snails, parboiled, shelled and drained
1 cup chicken stock
4 medium large baking potatoes, freshly baked
2/3 cup lowfat cottage cheese, lowfat sour cream,
*   plain yogurt or buttermilk*
1/2 to 2/3 cup finely chopped, well drained, cooked
*   spinach or Swiss chard*
1/2 cup freshly grated Gruyère cheese
Salt and freshly ground white pepper to taste
Paprika

In a saucepan, boil snails in chicken stock 10 minutes. Drain, reserving stock. When cool enough to handle, chop snails coarsely and set aside.

Cut a thin slice off top of potatoes and carefully scoop out pulp, leaving a shell about 3/8 inch thick. Mash pulp while still hot and with fork stir in cottage cheese. Toss in spinach, reserved snails and 1/4 cup of Gruyère cheese. Season with salt and pepper and thin with reserved stock if potatoes are too stiff.

Mound mixture into reserved shells and place on baking sheet. Sprinkle with remaining cheese and dust with paprika. Bake in a preheated 350° F oven 15 minutes, or until heated through and lightly browned.

Snails Es-Car-Bor-Do-Lay

A new and unique marinade/sauce, Radich Bor-Do-Lay, is soon to be introduced into Safeway and other select markets. It imparts a delicious flavor to a variety of foods and is especially good with snails.
Serve this snail sauce over freshly cooked rice or pasta. With French bread, a salad, and a light dessert, your meal will be complete.

serves three or four

24 fresh snails, parboiled, shelled and drained
4 tablespoons unsalted butter
6 to eight large cloves garlic, minced
1/2 cup Radich Bor-Do-Lay marinade
10 sprigs fresh parsley, chopped
1/2 cup freshly grated Parmesan cheese
Cherry tomatoes

If large, slice snails in half. In a heavy skillet, heat butter and garlic until butter is melted. Add snails, cover and simmer 10 minutes. Do not let butter brown. Add Bor-Do-Lay sauce and parsley; cook until just heated through.

Pour snail mixture over rice or pasta and sprinkle with cheese. Garnish with tomatoes.

Garlic Snail Scrambled Eggs

A brunch or a special Sunday night supper would be the perfect time for these delicious eggs.

serves four

24 fresh snails, parboiled, shelled, drained and snipped in half
4 large fresh mushrooms, cleaned and chopped
3 cloves garlic, minced
1/4 cup coarsely chopped walnuts
1/4 cup extra virgin olive oil
8 large eggs
3 tablespoons water
3 tablespoons minced fresh parsley
1/2 teaspoon herb seasoning
1/4 teaspoon **each** *salt and freshly ground white pepper*
Canned mandarin orange sections
Watercress or parsley sprigs

In a large non-stick skillet, sauté snails, mushrooms, garlic and walnuts in oil 4 to 5 minutes, shaking skillet gently while cooking.

In a bowl, with a whisk, beat eggs, water, parsley and seasonings. Pour over snail mixture, shaking or stirring with a wooden spoon until blended. Cover and cook over low heat until lightly set. Tip pan while lifting cooked edges of eggs so uncooked egg flows onto bottom of skillet.

When eggs are cooked to taste, turn out onto warmed serving plates. Arrange orange sections around each serving and garnish each with a watercress sprig.

Index

Recipes/Notes

Recipes/Notes

Recipes/Notes

Recipes/Notes

Recipes / Notes